Freshening Breezes

FRESHENING BREEZES
FISHING BOATS OF CLEVELAND & NORTH YORKSHIRE

GLORIA WILSON

The
History
Press

Frontispiece: Galilee WY68 and *Prosperity* WY59 were built in Scotland in the 1930s for Whitby owners. At the start of the 1960s, they were still fishing from the Yorkshire port.

Cover illustrations: Front: Endeavour WY1, built by Reekie in 1934. *Back: Jane Elizabeth* WY144, built by Whitby Shipbuilding in 1960. (Both author)

First published 2013

The History Press
The Mill, Brimscombe Port
Stroud, Gloucestershire, GL5 2QG
www.thehistorypress.co.uk

British Library Cataloguing in Publication Data.
A catalogue record for this book is available from the British Library.

ISBN 978 0 7524 8041 1

Typesetting and origination by The History Press
Printed in Great Britain

CONTENTS

Completed in 1989, Skipper Shaun Elwick's 32ft 8in *Charisma* WY313 was one of the many well-liked cobles built by C.A. Goodall Boatbuilders at Sandsend near Whitby. She was powered by an 85hp diesel engine.

ACKNOWLEDGEMENTS

I would like to thank all those kindly and supportive people who provided the information which has enabled me to put this book together. It is impossible to mention them individually because there are so many. My involvement with the fishing communities has been a rewarding and happy experience.

AUTHOR'S NOTE

Almost all the text and captions mention skippers by name. This should not imply that they were necessarily sole owners of the vessels. Often family members, crewmen, fish-selling companies and others would own shares, and in one or two instances, the boats were wholly owned by shore-based interests.

It would be too wordy to mention all owners by name and could perhaps be intrusive.

Imperial measurements are used in much of the book. All but the newer boats were built in pre-metric days.

INTRODUCTION

The 24-mile stretch of coastal north-east England, which lies between the Rivers Tees and Esk, displays a remarkable diversity of character; from the sandy beach and seaside resort of Redcar in heavily industrialised Teesside, to the precipitous high cliffs and the enchanting historic fishing ports of Staithes and Whitby to the south-east.

The cliffs are of Jurassic rock overlaid with boulder clay. Treacherous rocky outcrops, known locally as 'scars', lie at their feet and further offshore. Prevailing winds are south-westerly, but strong easterly gales transform the coast into an inhospitable lee shore with heavy breakers and surf that reach far out to sea. Countless craft have foundered on these scars, or in the horrendous seas at the foot of the high cliffs. A thick sea mist, or 'roke', is also a particular hazard hereabouts. Even in good conditions fishermen must take care to locate the exact approach to a landing place, such as the difficult channels through the long, perilous scars, which extend from the beach at Redcar.

The North Sea is amongst the richest fishing grounds of all continental shelves. White fish such as cod, haddock, ling and plaice, and also lobster, brown crab, migratory salmon and herring have been fished extensively.

This book sets out to illustrate some of the fishing boats that have been built and owned in various places along this coastline. Fishermen have chosen a variety of craft to meet wide local circumstances and fishing requirements. Though touching upon subjects covered in the author's earlier publication, *Fishing Boats of Whitby and District* (Hutton Press Ltd, 1998), this new book is very much more a visual appraisal, using many more photographs and offering new information.

Apart from making a few forays into things historical, the author has drawn on her own experience and original fieldwork, and has taken all the photographs, so the book cannot pretend to be exhaustive. It concentrates largely on the modern era, from sometime around the 1950s to the start of the twenty-first century, with perhaps greater emphasis on some localities than on others. Each place has its own rich history, personality and powerful local identity.

With a notional population of 1,000 in the late eighteenth and early nineteenth centuries, Staithes achieved importance as a fishing port far greater than its size and became the most significant fishing station on the English coast, north of the Wash. In 1817, it owned some seventy cobles and fourteen sturdy Yorkshire luggers. In February and March the luggers began line fishing, primarily for cod, ling, haddock and turbot, close to the Dogger Bank. Fishing was done from two cobles, which the bigger boat carried to sea on her deck. Later in the year, the luggers took part in the East Anglian herring drift-net fishery. Fishing may not have been their sole occupation, however. Smuggling of dutiable goods, including spirits, lace, tea, tobacco and silk, was rife in Staithes prior to 1820 or thereabouts. Customs officers kept an eye on these luggers, and for good reason: at least one Staithes lugger had a false bulkhead behind which contraband could be hidden. Said to be superb sea boats, the luggers could handle heavy weather. Waves broke dangerously on the shallow Dogger Bank.

Later, a vigorous Yorkshire herring fishery developed, which, by the late 1850s, was amongst the most profitable in Great Britain. For much of the nineteenth century, Staithes owned as many as a hundred cobles. In the early 1860s, for instance, some forty cobles worked longlines from November until March, 6–10 miles offshore on hard, rocky ground.

Though at various times a fishing port of some consequence, Whitby prospered particularly during the eighteenth and early nineteenth centuries through shipbuilding and repairing, ship owning, and whaling. In 1792–93 it was the second-most important merchant ship-building town in England for the tonnage of shipping produced. Captain James Cook's vessels of exploration and scientific investigation, *Endeavour* and *Resolution*, were in fact converted Whitby-built colliers: rugged, bluff bowed and flat bottomed with excellent handling, sea keeping and beaching qualities. Cook (1728–79) had sailed on Whitby ships before joining the Royal Navy in 1755.

Whitby was ideally placed to build sailing colliers for the coal trade from Northumberland and Durham, to London and the south-east. Industrial activity in much of the region was unparalleled in the nineteenth and early twentieth centuries. With its proximity to coal from Durham and iron ore from the

Cleveland and Eston hills, the River Tees became an iron and steel, shipbuilding and engineering centre of worldwide significance. In the 1940s, Imperial Chemical Industries established a huge plastics and petro-chemical manufacturing facility at Wilton. The last of the ironstone mines closed in 1964 but steel and petro-chemicals remained important. At the close of the twentieth century there was considerable seaborne trade, with ships annually bringing some 5½ million tonnes of iron ore and scrap to the huge Corus steelmaking plant at Redcar.

Tourism developed everywhere. Redcar was one of the few places where white fish and shellfish were sold directly from the fishing vessels. Small knots of customers queued up alongside the boats on the seafront against a background of amusement arcades, cafes and gift shops, bingo halls, children's roundabouts and huge inflatable octopi. The rising and falling voice of the bingo caller sounded like Gregorian chant, and ice cream topped with lemon sorbet became a local speciality.

⚓ ⚓ ⚓

For many, there is one outstanding boat associated with the fishing communities of north-east England: the curiously shaped English square-sterned coble. In addition to being a splendid sea boat, she is ideal for launch and recovery, stern to shore, through heavy-breaking surf. The coble can also negotiate rollers and shallow-breaking seas when entering and leaving unsheltered tidal harbours and creeks.

Forward and after parts differ in shape remarkably. She has pronounced forward sheer with high, slightly curved forward-raking stem and uncommonly deep, rounded forefoot. Her entry is fine with lean hollow lines below the waterline and considerable flare and shoulder above. Forming a continuation of the forefoot, the part-keel ends just abaft amidships. The entry is sufficiently fine to cut through the water, whilst the flare and shoulder give lift in heavy seas and buoyancy when heeling. The deep forefoot, lean entry and hollow underwater lines grip the seas for windward sailing.

When the coble is putting to sea or making a landing, the full flare and shoulders lift her head so that she is not overwhelmed by the waves and, together with the high bow, they prevent water breaking inboard. At the water's edge the deep forefoot, sharp entry and hollow underwater lines help keep her head to sea, and the forefoot digs into the sand and steadies the coble during retrieval. She has a shallow afterbody with flat floors and hard bilges. Two side keels or drafts extend from just forward of amidships to the stern. They facilitate launching and beaching, prevent her after end from digging into the sand, and hold her upright when ashore.

Strakes are broad, and for much of its length the sheerstrake has a generous tumblehome, which increases the degree to which the coble can heel before water falls inboard. The horseshoe-shaped square stern rakes aft at some 45 degrees, and the very long rudder functions as a deep keel to grip the water.

All these characteristics enable the coble to be beached, rowed and sailed, and to adapt readily to motor power. Sailing coble rig was simple, normally comprising single large dipping lugsail, which could be lowered quickly in a squall. By the 1940s the majority of cobles had an engine, positioned forward of amidships to keep the shaft angle low and retain the boat's shallowness aft. The propeller was housed between the drafts to shield it from damage.

There has long been another type of small, open boat working alongside the coble, however: less widely known perhaps, used for commercial and pleasure fishing along this harsh coast, and in some places outnumbering the coble and known locally as a 'double-ender'. Although double-ender is a generic term for any vessel pointed at both ends, it refers along this coastline to a very specific type of craft. In fact, some fishermen just call her a 'boat' in order to differentiate her from a coble.

Many fishermen find the double-ender handier than a coble for working the lively waters close to the cliffs and for crossing the surf. She is quite different from the coble. Most particularly, she is usually smaller and is launched and recovered with her bows into shore. Measuring between 14ft and 26ft long overall, with a length to beam ratio of 3:1, the double-ender is similar in form at both ends. Pointed at stem and sternpost, she has a full-length keel and flat floors, and usually has steam-bent timbers. Her rounded sections are created by the use of many more and narrower planks than those built into the more angular coble. A double-ender can be remarkably pretty if her strakes are fair and eyesweet all the way.

Though some would argue that the coble makes a superior sea boat and can work in worse weather, cobles and double-enders appear more or less equally fitted for similar purposes in the broad local conditions. Boat builders have produced both types with equal finesse; both are adaptable and can fish for different species, switching easily to alternative fishing methods according to season and opportunity.

Much more research is needed if we are to learn the pre-nineteenth century ancestry of the double-ender. Many maritime writers have described the coble but writings on the double-ender are sparse. We do know there were many builders of double-enders throughout the region, with each developing his own style based on experience, imagination and the needs of the fishermen. J.N. Lowther & Co. (Whitby) Ltd built a full-bodied stalwart type that carried her fullness well forward and aft. William Clarkson (Whitby) Ltd often produced a sprightlier boat, finer at the ends and slacker in the bilge, and sometimes characterised by a steeply raked stern.

Certain facets of double-ender design are predetermined. For good surf-riding characteristics, she should have her centre of gravity as far aft as possible. Her forebody should have excellent reserve buoyancy. She needs to have sensitive steering and good directional stability to minimise the risk of broaching, and her draught must be shallow to keep her afloat near the beach.

On the other hand, much larger craft of entirely different concept have proved suitable for working from Whitby. Between 1930 and the turn of the twenty-first century, more than fifty new or second-hand Scottish-built vessels belonged to the Yorkshire port, with fishermen obtaining replacements when design advanced or fishing methods changed. They were locally called 'keelboats', most probably to distinguish them from the part-keeled cobles.

Between the two world wars, Whitby acquired fully decked, carvel-planked motor fifies and half-zulus, which, compared to cobles, were able to make longer trips further afield in worse weather and deeper water, and could handle more fishing gear. They had evolved from the Scottish east coast lug-rigged double-ended sailing fifies and zulus but were generally smaller and not so deep, with flatter floors and harder bilges, and the rounded forefoot gave greater manoeuvrability. They had a small wheelhouse and a mizzen steadying-sail, and were fuller and more buoyant aft to accommodate a petrol-paraffin or a diesel engine. Motor fifies had a near vertical sternpost. Motor half-zulus had a somewhat raking sternpost, but without the pronounced rake of the true zulu stern.

Motor half-zulu *Galilee* WY68 was built by the Stephen yard at Macduff in 1932 for Whitby owners. Opinions can vary, however, as to what degree of rake actually forms a half-zulu stern. There are those who would describe *Galilee* as a motor fifie with a slightly raking stern. *Galilee* was 44ft long with 14ft beam and powered by a Kelvin K2 two-cylinder 44hp diesel engine. *Prosperity* WY59, built for Whitby in 1935 by Walter Reekie at St Monans, was a true motor fifie with a more upright sternpost.

Canoe-sterned keelboats, similar to Scottish herring ring-netters, also came to Whitby in the inter-war years. Ring-netters needed to be light and manoeuvrable, and speedy with a quick and tight turn, so they had shallow draught and rounded forefoot, an easy entry and a clean run. The propeller aperture and rudder were tucked well beneath the buoyant canoe stern to avoid entanglement with the fishing gear. *Endeavour* WY1, built in 1934 by Walter Reekie at his Anstruther yard, measured 46ft with 14ft 6in beam and had a three-cylinder 52hp Ruston & Hornsby diesel engine, and a belt-driven capstan for hauling fishing gear. All these Scottish-built boats were handy and adaptable, and able to work herring drift-nets, herring ring-nets, longlines and crab and lobster pots.

Echo sounders and position finders made it possible to hunt and find fish more accurately. Following the Second World War, Whitby fishermen bought larger, more powerful, fuller-bodied cruiser-sterned keelboats with greater deck space and bigger wheelhouses, for Scottish flydragging seine-netting and inshore trawling for white fish. Cruiser-sterned *Success* KY211 for instance, delivered from Smith & Hutton (Boatbuilders) Ltd at Anstruther in 1960 to Skipper James Leadley, measured 55ft by 17ft. She was equipped with a Gardner 114hp diesel engine, mechanically driven winch and seine-net rope coiler, radiotelephone, echo sounder and Decca navigator. Though in her first year she worked seine-nets, herring drift-nets, longlines and crab and lobster pots, she later switched to full-time seine-net fishing and trawling. In dark weather, trawling was more productive than seining and could be done over rocky ground.

As time went on, keelboats became heftier and more powerful in order to pull increasingly robust trawling gear over much rougher stretches of seabed. Many had a transom stern, which afforded more space aft. The use of hydraulic rather than mechanical power for winches then gave greater flexibility and efficiency in working the fishing gear, and led to the use of the power block for lifting nets aboard.

1

STAITHES

Situated some 10 miles to the north-west of Whitby, the storm-battered village of Staithes is built on the sides of a deep ravine where Roxby beck runs into the sea between two immense cliffs. Tightly grouped houses are set every which way, around yards, slopes and alleyways, and there are very many steps.

All manner of things in Staithes are influenced by the sea and fishing. Some houses are named after boats, for instance Star of Hope Cottage, Confidence Cottage, Unity House, Blue Jacket House, Venus Cottage and Wavelet. Fishing paraphernalia and parts of boats have been used as house-building materials. Masts and spars support roofs and ceilings and, in 1998, in a house being renovated, the staves of fish barrels were even found covering a hole in the rafters.

Staithes is notable for several reasons. Circumnavigator and explorer Captain James Cook RN was employed for about eighteen months in the village in 1745–46, before moving to Whitby. Artists have always been fascinated by the locality and the Staithes Group, based in the area around the turn of the twentieth century, typified the best in British Impressionist painting.

Staithes lost its eminence as a great fishing port. By 1860 a large-scale trawl fishery for white fish was well established, particularly from Hull and Scarborough, though smaller ports including Staithes deplored the method. Line fishermen held trawlers responsible for depleting fish stocks, killing spawn, carrying away lines and undercutting the price of fish. Herring fishing was also threatened. Trawlers were claimed to kill herring spawn and cut the drift-nets, and French herring fishermen with stronger boats and nets forced the Staithes drifters off the grounds; they also worked on Sunday, which the deeply religious and chapel-going Staithes men did not.

Many Staithes men left fishing and found employment in the local ironstone mines. Some activity continued: fisherman Matthew Verrill told the author that a dozen cobles were still fishing from Staithes when he first went to sea in the coble *Star of Hope* WY174 in 1928. During the 1920s, several cobles worked herring drift-nets in addition to longlines and crab and lobster pots.

Following the close of the Second World War, fishing from Staithes was at a low ebb, and in 1950 only the coble *Star of Hope* WY174 and one or two double-enders worked crab and lobster pots between March and November, and stayed ashore for the remainder of the year. The availability of secure jobs, particularly in the nearby steel and chemical industries, offered attractive alternatives to the uncertainties of catching fish.

There was a new interest in fishing as the 1950s progressed, stimulated in part by government financial assistance for the purchase of new boats and engines. Three motor cobles were built for Staithes early in that decade.

Staithes has a townscape character of outstanding quality. It lies within the North York Moors National Park, on the 36-mile North Yorkshire & Cleveland Heritage Coast and on the 109-mile Cleveland Way.

During the 1970s there was a greater appreciation of the nutritional value of fish, and British fishermen enjoyed big earnings. All species fetched high prices. This prompted huge investment in new boats, and the increase in fishing effort also reflected the general expansion of Britain's coastal fisheries following the extension in 1964 of territorial limits from 3 to 12 miles.

In 1972 Staithes was the tenth highest port in England and Wales for the weight of lobsters put ashore. The arrival early in 1973 of the new cobles *Deep Harmony* WY86 and *Endurance* WY89 brought the strength of the Staithes coble fleet to six, the highest number since before the Second World War. Together with a dozen or so double-enders, the Staithes cobles worked whichever type of gear brought best results: crab and lobster pots, longlines, trammel and gill nets. Some were licensed to use drift-nets for salmon and sea trout, and at least one coble worked a small white fish trawl.

During the 1950s Britain had begun to recover from the drab and austere years following the Second World War. Work was plentiful and people felt hopeful and optimistic. There was a new interest in fishing, stimulated in part by the White Fish Authority's grant and loan scheme, which helped fishermen buy new boats and engines.

In 1953 two half-decked motor cobles, *Golden Crown* WY78 and *Coronation Queen* WY75, were built for Staithes. *Golden Crown* was built by William Clarkson (Whitby) Ltd for Richard, Matthew and Francis Verrill. She replaced the coble *Star of Hope* WY174, which had been wrecked in the great North Sea storm of 31 January 1953 when huge seas pounded the village and the Cod & Lobster pub was partly washed away. *Coronation Queen* was constructed by J. and J. Harrison at Amble and fished under William and George Harrison, and another Richard Verrill. Following village custom when a new boat arrived, both cobles were welcomed by cheering crowds lining the waterfront. Hand bells were rung and Staithes 'coble cake' was eaten in celebration.

Measuring 30ft 5in with 8ft 6in beam, *Golden Crown* was powered by a Petter AV2M two-cylinder 10hp 1,500rpm water-cooled diesel engine with 2:1 reduction gear. Her propeller was housed in a raised ram tunnel consisting of a hollowness in the sweep of the planking between the drafts. This feature was originated in the 1930s by William Clarkson.

Coronation Queen was 30ft long with 8ft 3in beam and had a Kelvin 15hp petrol-paraffin motor, with the propeller housed in a box tunnel formed over a cut-away area in the bottom planking. She was equipped with an auxiliary lugsail. Each coble had a hydraulic pot hauler. The two cobles were eventually sold away from Staithes.

A wave breaks near the Cod & Lobster public house. Staithes was often storm-drenched: heavy breakers and surf regularly rushed into the harbour and crashed against the buildings; water poured down chimneys. In the late twentieth century, sea defences in the form of rock armour were placed on the seaward side of the breakwaters.

Golden Crown was of broadish build and somewhat full at shoulders and quarters, with a strong sheer aft, a pronounced tumblehome and a broad bottom, and her relatively deep drafts were set well apart. Cobles built in Whitby and district had their own style: generally full-bodied with a lot of tumblehome and a good shoulder, and fairly hard in the bilge. Cobles from J. and J. Harrison were generally sleeker and leaner in hull form. Founded in 1870, the firm built more than 300 cobles, the majority for Northumberland owners who usually preferred a finer-lined, more rakish coble to the chunkier Yorkshire craft. And so, compared to *Golden Crown*, *Coronation Queen* looked somewhat slighter and sprightlier, with less sheer and softer bilges.

These crab and lobster pots have just been brought ashore. By the start of the 1980s, the cobles worked as many as 250–300 pots each.

Opposite above: Substantial snowfalls along the Yorkshire coast are associated with north-easterly winds off the North Sea. Staithes is not 'pretty-pretty' but has a grandeur with its high cliffs and densely packed tall dwellings.

Opposite below: Coronation Queen (left) and *Golden Crown* lie at low tide in the beck early in 1958 following heavy snow. The little double-ender in the background is the 19ft *Merina* WY19, owned by the author's father and built in the 1940s by Whitby Boatbuilding & Repairing Co.

Golden Crown and *Coronation Queen* were half-decked to provide shelter when lying-to at the longline fishing or waiting to enter the tidal harbour, and to give cover for the engine. They fished with longlines in the winter, chiefly for cod, and each worked about 150 crab and lobster pots from spring until autumn.

Golden Crown sits on the beach. She was highly thought of as a grand little sea boat and was good at running before the wind.

Skipper George Hanson sits at the tiller of the 31ft coble *Sea Lover* WY99, delivered in 1954 from J. and J. Harrison. She had a Kelvin 15hp petrol-paraffin engine. In 1957, George tragically died after saving the life of a boy in difficulties in the harbour at Staithes and attempting to rescue a man. *Sea Lover* was later sold to Redcar owners.

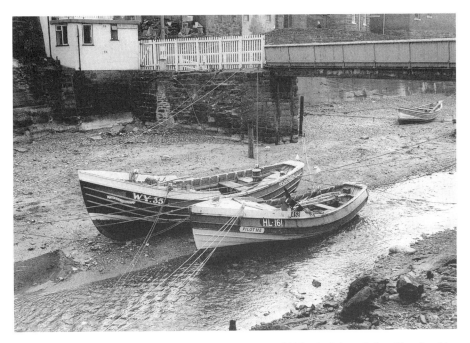

Ocean Queen WY35 (left) was an early example of the full-bodied, broad-shouldered cobles built by C.A. Goodall Boatbuilder at Sandsend near Whitby. Master boat builder 'Tony' Goodall said, 'We considered that a fuller sturdy lined coble was needed when motors got bigger. If she is too fine she will take off in a following sea and broach to. A fuller lined coble will hold her head up and surf along the top. Also the fishermen wanted a fuller coble to carry more fishing gear.'

Built in 1971 for Skipper William Harrison, the 28ft 6in by 9ft 6in *Ocean Queen* had a Lister 44.25hp diesel engine with 2:1 reduction ratio. *Ocean Queen* carried a hydraulically powered pot hauler, and one of the first fully transistorised echo sounders from Kelvin Hughes, the MS39, which was well liked for small vessels. The trimmer, slighter *Pilot Me* HL161, built by Harrison in the 1940s, was brought to Staithes by Skipper William Blackwell.

Deep Harmony WY86 lies in the tidal beck. Handed over from Goodall in 1973 to Skipper Harry Hogarth, she was 28ft 3in long but was not quite as capacious as *Ocean Queen*. Many cobles were by now carrying more machinery for hauling fishing gear, and *Deep Harmony* carried a hydraulically driven pot hauler and trawl winch. *Deep Harmony* was powered by a Lister 44.25hp 2,200rpm diesel motor with 2:1 reduction gearbox. Reduction gearing was desirable in order to make the propeller more efficient. Larger diameter, slower-turning propellers gave better control and manoeuvrability to relatively slow and heavy craft such as fishing vessels. *Deep Harmony* was also fitted with a Ferrograph G500 echo sounder, which was becoming widely used by coble fishermen for navigation, fish finding and pinpointing wrecks.

Deep Harmony is launched following an overhaul at her builder's yard. She used 300 crab and lobster pots and sometimes trawled to catch small fish for use as pot bait. On occasion, she trawled for quality marketable species such as soles.

Ocean Queen
WY35 was
shorter and
beamier
than Skipper
William
Harrison's
earlier coble
*Coronation
Queen* WY75,
and more full
bodied.

In 1973 Gordon Clarkson Boatbuilder in Whitby built the beamy curvaceous full-bodied coble *Endurance* WY89 for Skipper Arthur England. The purpose of her buxom shape was to produce a roomy coble within the overall length of 30ft; small enough to be handled up the beck by two crewmen and not occupy too much space at the moorings. *Endurance* had a 65hp 2,400rpm Ford diesel engine with 2:1 reduction ratio and carried a hydraulic pot hauler and an echo sounder.

Measuring 9ft 6in on the beam, *Endurance* was of larch on oak construction. Her Model 300 pot hauler from North Sea Winches of Scarborough was driven via a small hydraulic pump from the forward end of the engine.

Endurance sits on the coble grid between tides for a scrub and anti-fouling. Her builder Gordon Clarkson said, 'She was particularly full and beamy with full bilge and strong sheer and a robust tumblehome.'

Above: Half-decked Staithes coble *Star of Hope* WY223 lies in Tony Goodall's premises in the 1970s following an overhaul. Built by J. and J. Harrison in 1965 for Skipper Matthew Verrill, the 31ft craft had a Petter 33.75hp motor. Harrison's master boat builder Hector Handyside said that she was the first Harrison coble to have a Whitby-style raised ram tunnel, made by bending the bottom planking into a concavity between the drafts. Matt had been part owner of *Golden Crown* WY78 and was happy with the efficiency of her tunnel, which gave a good, smooth water flow around the propeller. During the 1970s *Star of Hope* worked 350 crab and lobster pots and six longlines, each line being 360 fathoms long and bearing haddock hooks on 3ft 'snoods' at 9ft intervals.

Below: At 27ft 6in long, the coble *Embrace* WY207 was built in the early 1960s by Gordon Clarkson for Skipper George Harrison and was designed for beaching with deepish drafts to protect her propeller. Her 22hp Petter diesel engine was air cooled to enable it to be started before she entered the water. *Endurance* WY89 lies on the other side of *Star of Hope* WY223.

Opposite above: The same three cobles face a bit of a swell, which is coming into the beck at high tide. Plenty of good mooring ropes are necessary.

Opposite below: Mrs Edith Marsay sorts crabs after they have been boiled. Yorkshire crabs are often small but have a high meat content.

Staithes was not a tidy place but it was all the better for this. The paraphernalia of fishing gear added much to the essence and character of the village.

In 1973 Skipper Matt Verrill (right) and crewman Leonard Cole of *Star of Hope* WY223 rig pots ready for taking to sea.

Opposite above: Here enjoying the sun are, from left to right: Richard (Dickie) Verrill, Elizabeth Verrill, Francis (Tange) Verrill and Harold Armstrong. Tange's attractive collie sits in attendance.

Opposite below: Pilot Me B WY216, built by J.N. Lowther & Co. (Whitby) Ltd for Skipper Bill Blackwell in 1975, was slimmer forward than the characteristic Whitby-style coble. Bill said, 'I asked for a finer bow to cut through the water more cleanly when going into the wind and so that she would not bounce up and down so much.' Measuring 28ft long, she had a Mercedes 45hp engine.

Opposite above: At 26ft long, *All My Sons* WY267 was a smallish coble built by William Clarkson in 1976 for Skipper Ian Baxter. Powered by a Mercedes 36hp diesel engine with 2:1 reduction gear, she carried pot and line hauler, echo sounder and radiotelephone.

Opposite below: In 1977, Gordon Clarkson built the 30ft coble *Embrace G* WY278 for Skipper George Harrison. Although of similar beam to *Endurance* WY89, she was less bluff forward and was powered by a Petter 33.75hp diesel engine with 2:1 reduction ratio. Despite being somewhat too big and heavy to work from the beach easily, she could at a pinch be hauled ashore. The line of her keel was carried aft along the drafts to allow her to move smoothly over the launching boards. She carried an echo sounder, handy in fog for locating wrecks and hard ground. *Embrace G* worked crab and lobster pots, longlines and gill and trammel nets. She had a licence to use drift-nets during the summer salmon and trout fishery, which happily came at a time when lobsters were casting their shells and were of poor quality.

Fishermen John Cole (left) and Simon Theaker prepare longlines using mussels for bait. Lines were coiled on an oval wickerwork basket called a skep. Codling and a few haddocks were the main fish caught.

Opposite: Skipper Bill Blackwell (left) of *Pilot Me B* WY216 with baiter John Hambley get longlines ready for sea. Bill's warehouse was formerly a boat builder's premises.

Pilot Me B WY216 prepares for the potting season.

Down in the harbour at Staithes the tide is out. Stalwart coble *Endurance* WY89 had very full and curvy lines.

Opposite above: Skipper Raymond Marsay's 31ft coble *Crystal Sea* WY296 was built in the late 1970s by Gordon Clarkson.

Opposite below: Crystal Sea was one of the final cobles built by Gordon Clarkson, who had set up business in 1950.

Seen from Cowbar Nab, Staithes presents a townscape set at all levels. Cobles lie in the beck with their bows facing towards the harbour and sea, whereas double-enders face landwards. The tide is out.

Opposite above: Staithes is strong in character, full of lively, unusual visual incidents and surprises.

Opposite below: Bonny 26ft by 8ft 6in double-ender *Seaton Rose* WY310 and the small pretty coble *Eventide A* WY203 were built by Tony Goodall. Constructed in 1979 for Skipper Frank Hanson and his son David, *Seaton Rose* has superb lines. At 27ft long the beach coble *Eventide A* had been built in the mid-1970s and later bought by Staithes fishermen Duncan Major and John Dawson.

Seaton Rose was robustly constructed. In preference to steamed and bent timbers, she had stout sawn oak frames similar to those in a coble. Her owners chose a double-ender rather than a coble as they felt that she would be more suitable for working two-handed.

Opposite: Seaton Rose was powered by a Lister three-cylinder 44hp 2,200rpm engine with 2:1 reduction gearbox. Other fittings included hydraulically powered pot and line hauler, gill and trammel net hauler, and Ferrograph G500 echo sounder.

Above: These double-enders vary in shape in accordance with their builders' individual styles and their owners' preferences. A couple of cobles and the odd small, square-sterned boat are among them.

Below: J.N. Lowther produced beamy, buxom, spacious, full-bodied double-enders. Their shoulders and quarters were equally and exceptionally full so that they would not run away on a sea. *Jubilee Queen* WY174, owned by Skipper Duncan Major, was characteristic of this.

2

WHITBY – PART 1

Clustered around a splendid natural harbour formed by the River Esk, which flows into the North Sea between craggy cliffs some 200ft high, is Whitby, standing proud beneath the gaunt, windswept abbey of St Hilda.

Much of Whitby's atmosphere and charm lies in the complexity of its layout, with pantiled dwellings built on all levels on sloping, uneven ground, tightly packed along narrow thoroughfares and yards, and often only reached by passageways and precipitous flights of steps. The town bristles with intriguing names – Argument's Yard, New Way Ghaut, Salt Pan Well Steps and Loggerheads Yard – and part of the harbour is known as Abraham's Bosom. It can be cold and desolate in winter, however, wracked by bitter winds and snowstorms. The harbour entrance is exposed to strong winds from the north-west through north to north-east and, in more than a Force 6 wind, dangerous breaking seas can pound between the arms of the entrance piers.

There was big herring fishing in the 1940s and '50s. Tremendous shoals had built up during the Second World War and markets for herring were on the rise. Over 100 Scottish ring-netters and drifters were based at Whitby during the Yorkshire herring season, from July to October, and local vessels also took part. The two fishing methods had advantages and drawbacks. In rough weather and strong tides, it was difficult to operate ring-nets and transfer crews from one boat to another (ring-netters worked in pairs). Drifters preferred a full moon and could fish in worse weather and spring tides. Although the Whitby men did some ring-netting, they thought herring caught by drift-net was of superior quality because it was not mixed up with a mess of spawn and scales. Drift-nets were hung vertically like a curtain in the path of the herring shoals.

In the late 1950s the author enjoyed a trip to the herring grounds with the 52ft cruiser-sterned keelboat *Lead Us II* A291. A fleet of twenty drift-nets was used, whereas the bigger Scottish drifters fished eighty or so. The trip was full of delightful sights, with moonlight and green phosphorescence, and everyone covered in thousands of opalescent herring scales that filled the air as the fishermen hauled the fishing gear and shook the fish out of the nets onto the deck. Later there was fog, and a cacophony of warning honks, whistles, booms and wheezes sounded from dozens of nearby drifters and ring-netters.

But herring shoals dwindled, landings at Whitby falling to virtually nothing by the 1970s. Fishermen concentrated on other species. Towards the close of the 1960s, Whitby's full-time fishing fleet largely comprised about a dozen cobles and twelve keelboats, the majority of which had joined the fleet since 1957. Though one or two keelboats worked crab and lobster pots, the majority caught white fish with trawls and flydragging seine-nets, staying at sea for one day. Whitby fish was, therefore, very fresh and, being well washed and packed in flake ice, it was renowned for its high quality. Landings of white fish, mainly cod, haddock, plaice and whiting, had increased annually from 9,755cwt in 1957 to 36,096cwt in 1967, owing to the build-up of this modern fleet of seining and trawling keelboats. Herring was by now so scarce that in 1968 only one local keelboat, *Ocean Venture* KY209, worked drift-nets for a few weeks. Over-fishing, blamed largely on Scottish and European mid-water trawlers and purse-seiners, led to a moratorium on North Sea herring fishing from 1977 to 1981. Many marketing outlets were consequently lost.

By the closing years of the twentieth century, Whitby had become primarily a holiday and tourist town. Nevertheless, it also survived as a small but much-respected fishing, boat building and fish processing port with a fleet of some forty boats landing quality fish, which attracted high prices at auction. Statistics provided by the then Ministry of Agriculture, Fisheries and Food show that Whitby landings of white fish and shellfish during 1998 amounted to 4,668 tonnes, which sold for £4,947,535. Of this, some 2,713 tonnes were cod, whilst the next most plentiful species were whiting, haddock and lemon sole. The figures placed Whitby as the fourth most important fishing town on the English east coast for the value of fish landed by UK vessels. It was beaten only by Grimsby, Hull and Lowestoft.

Though cod, haddock and whiting remained the mainstay for Whitby trawlers, there was a greater spread of fishing activity as the 1990s progressed. Two or three trawlers began to catch prime monkfish, lemon sole and plaice on soft ground in Scottish waters. Later in the 1990s, a growing number made weekly trips into the northern North Sea using heavy 'rockhopper' trawls 350 miles or more from home, to fish off Shetland and around the oil fields and pipelines. They brought back ling, saithe, tusk, pollack, catfish and redfish, as well as much cod and had-dock, thereby spreading the variety of species being sold on Whitby fish market.

One or two boats braved strong tides and shifting sands to target cod in the Thames estuary. *Sophie Louise* WY168 and others caught valuable red mullet off the Dutch, German and Belgian coastlines. In addition, around the turn of the millennium at least one boat used twin-rig gear for plaice and lemon sole on the southern Dogger Bank. Others made their first serious attempts at the prawn (*Nephrops*) fishing at the Silver Pitts. Arnold Locker, Director of Lockers Trawlers Ltd, said, 'Whitby as a port has many different fishings to change over to and explore, such as red mullet and plaice and now the prawn fishing and we're getting better at it each year.'

Yet few years were alike. A prolific and lucrative cod fishery just off the Yorkshire coast in 1998 temporarily returned Whitby to its traditional role as a predominantly inshore port. Dave Winspear, director of fish-selling agency Alliance Fish (Whitby) Ltd, said, 'It was a happy time when quality fish met a consistent demand.'

The majority of Whitby's fleet of some sixteen trawlers at the close of the 1990s measured less than 60ft long overall. A bylaw permitted vessels of not more than 60ft overall to trawl in certain local coastal waters prohibited to bigger boats. It was most important to Whitby fishermen that their trawlers had good towing capabilities. Their design and propulsion characteristics needed to allow them to pull heavy, robust fishing gear over exceptionally craggy ground. They also needed to give them a firm grip in the water in order to keep the net in position, so that it continued to fish effectively and did not collapse or flap about.

For much of the late 1990s, a busy and bustling fleet of about twenty static gear boats less than 33ft long overall worked, variously, crab and lobster pots, gill and trammel nets, longlines and salmon drift and beach nets. They included some half dozen cobles, popular with Whitby fishermen for being good little sea boats and able to work fishing gear close inshore among the stones. Static gear boats tried different things at various times, too. One or two caught turbot with shallow gill nets left for three days near to wrecks. The big run of cod in 1998 was beneficial to the static gear fleet and, one week, the mini keelboat *Rose Anne* WY164 caught a mighty 900 stones of that species in her trammel nets.

Whitby never recovered as a herring port. In the late 1990s, huge Scottish purse-seiners and mid-water trawlers 60–70m long were landing herring and mackerel to processing plants in Scotland and Norway.

Whitby fishermen wish to have a sustainable and profitable future. They deplore the European Union Common Fisheries Policy for its incredibly bureaucratic and centralised approach to the management of such a diverse and complex industry. In particular, the quota system is a problem in mixed fisheries where many types of fish are caught. Over-quota species caught by accident must be dumped overboard, dead. Fishermen would much prefer the fisheries and conservation policies to be managed on a regional basis, geared to individual needs and circumstances.

The Dock End in Whitby's upper harbour provided good shelter for the fishing boats. Keelboat *Wakeful* KY261 was delivered in 1960 from Scottish builder James N. Miller & Sons Ltd at St Monans.

Opposite above: Keelboats *Whitby Rose* WY110, *Endeavour* WY1 and *Success* KY211 lie in the Dock End in the early 1960s. Work is under way in the background building Endeavour Wharf to provide facilities for loading and discharging cargo ships.

Opposite below: There are those who would regard *Galilee* WY68 as a motor half-zulu because her stern rakes somewhat, unlike the almost vertical stern of the true motor fifie. Built by the Stephen yard at Macduff in 1932 for Skipper Edward Verrill, she was the seventeenth fishing boat to have a Kelvin diesel engine. Note her rudder, mizzen steadying sail and galley chimney.

Opposite: Built in 1935 by Walter Reekie at his Anstruther yard for Skipper Henry Duke, *Easter Morn* WY61 was a 42ft-long motor fifie powered by a Kelvin 44hp diesel engine. She pioneered the use in Whitby of the Hyland hydraulically powered pot hauler.

Sammy Winspear, who sailed with *Galilee* for twenty-six years, said her fishing activities included potting, longlining, and some herring drifting and ring-net fishing. Big strong overlines with herring bait on large hooks were also fished in deep water some 50 miles away for turbot, cod and ling.

Opposite above: A true motor fifie with virtually upright stern, the 42ft *Prosperity* WY59 was delivered in 1935 from Walter Reekie's St Monans yard to Skipper J. Dryden. She was powered by a Ruston & Hornsby 36hp diesel engine.

Opposite below: Of similar type to *Galilee*, *Venus* WY67 was built by Stephen in 1932 for Skipper James Cole. At 43ft with 13ft beam, she cost some £800 to build.

Venus was one of some twenty-five boats built in 1932 at the Stephen yard. Boat builders all along the Moray Firth coast were working hectically to produce motor-driven craft, which, in Scotland, were replacing the steam-powered herring drifters that were too costly to operate. Whitby men liked these motor vessels too.

Opposite: In the early 1960s, *Prosperity* still worked out of Whitby. Note her rudder and steering mechanism.

Endeavour WY1 was built in 1934 by Reekie at Anstruther for Skipper Thomas Hutchinson. Measuring 46ft with 14ft 6in beam, she had a three-cylinder 52hp Ruston & Hornsby diesel engine and belt-driven capstan. The buoyant canoe stern with rudder tucked underneath dispensed with the projecting fifie and half-zulu rudder, which had caused resistance when the boats were turning and became easily damaged or entangled with fishing gear.

Endeavour's last skipper was Matthew Hutchinson who joined his father, Matt Snr, in 1959. At various times she worked longlines, crab and lobster pots, and herring drift-nets. She also did some overing for turbot, using big hooks that were baited aboard the boat with herring or mackerel.

Opposite above: Matt Hutchinson Jnr said *Endeavour* was a lovely sea boat. He remembered, 'Once, in the early 1960s, we got caught in a 90-knot north-easterly gale and snow while shooting pots. It was heshing down with rain and snow and you couldn't see for snow and sea.'

Opposite below: Whitby Rose WY110, built by Whitby Boatbuilding & Repairing Co. in 1957 for Skipper Alf Locker, was similar to the classic Scottish canoe-sterned herring ring-netter with shallow draught and rounded forefoot, easy entry and clean run, with firm bilges to prevent excess rolling and give good carrying space. Measuring 50ft by 16ft, she had a Kelvin 88hp diesel motor.

Opposite above: Delivered from Whitby Boatbuilding in 1958 to Skipper William Graham, *Accord* WY130 had similar dimensions to *Whitby Rose* but was deeper with stronger sheer and heavier stern, and built with flydragging seine-netting in mind. Powered by a Kelvin 88hp motor, she cost some £13,500 to construct.

Opposite below: Scotland's oldest boatyard, James N. Miller & Sons Ltd at St Monans, founded in 1747, built several stalwart cruiser-sterned flydragging seine-netters for Whitby, featuring the bluff and flared Queen Mary bow, which gave more deck room forward for safer operation of the winch and ropes, and threw the water aside. A fuller, heavier afterbody gave more space aft and held the boat steadier in rough weather. *Wakeful* KY261, constructed in 1960 for Skipper George Storr, had these features and was 50ft long with a Gardner 114hp diesel engine.

During her latter years, *Wakeful*, affectionately known as 'Wakey', worked as a seiner and trawler. On a dismal morning in 1996 she was broken up under the infamous fishing boat decommissioning programme. One onlooker remarked, 'Poor old lass.'

Opposite above: Skipper Ronnie Frampton's small but sturdy 42ft by 15ft *Golden Hope* WY141 came from Miller in 1959 and was powered by a Kelvin 66hp diesel motor. Note the Queen Mary bow, with the stem having the aft siding greater than that at its face.

Opposite below: Built by Miller in 1959 for Scottish owners, *Ocean Venture* KY209 was later acquired by Whitby skipper Jack Hebden. At 55ft and powered by a Gardner 114hp engine, she was similar in shape to *Wakeful*. Though she did some herring drifting she later concentrated on the flydragging seine-net. She carried storage reels for the seine-net ropes.

Seine-netter *Achieve* WY155, delivered from Miller early in 1960 to Skipper Eric Taylor, was more akin to the firm's ring-netter design with leaner lines, trimmer stern and less flare to the bow. Measuring 49ft by 16.6ft, she was powered by a Gardner 96hp motor.

Opposite above: Crabs are sorted on board *Golden Hope* WY141. Large quantities of crabs are found where the seabed is of a rugged nature and, consequently, landings of crab at Whitby were considerable.

Opposite below: Fishermen, on board one of the older keelboats lying alongside the fish market in the early 1960s, are getting line-caught fish ready for hoisting ashore.

Skipper James Leadley's 55ft cruiser-sterned keelboat *Success* KY211 returns from a flydragging seine-netting trip. She was launched in April 1960 from Smith & Hutton (Boatbuilders) Ltd at Anstruther. During her first year she worked thirty-five to forty herring drift-nets, six longlines and 450 crab and lobster pots, in addition to seine-nets. In 1961 she switched to seining full-time, fishing up to 100 miles offshore. Line fishing was becoming uneconomical for the keelboats owing to the costs of gear and mussels as well as labour for baiting. Herring shoals were diminishing and high bait prices made potting unprofitable. In the storm-lashed winter of 1962/63, *Success* was equipped for white fish trawling. She then worked seine-nets during the summer and trawls in winter on rougher ground further inshore. The seabed off Whitby has many peaks and troughs.

Success had lovely eyesweet and pretty lines. Skipper James Leadley said, 'She takes some punishment. She's very good at running before a heavy following sea because she isn't too full aft.'

Opposite above: The cod end full of fish is lifted aboard *Success* during a flydragging seine-netting trip. Skipper James Leadley watches from the wheelhouse window.

Opposite below: Skipper Raymond Storr's 52ft by 16ft 6in keelboat *Lead Us II* A291 was built in 1959 by Whitby Shipbuilding and Engineering Co., formerly named Whitby Boatbuilding & Repairing Co. Turbulent seas can run into Whitby harbour, whose entrance faces north.

Opposite above: Lead Us II was a happy compromise between two hull types and was designed to be roomy with plenty of deck space as well as good herring-carrying capacity. Her full cruiser stern was inspired by those of buxom Danish anchor seine-netters, yet there were Scottish flydragging seiner influences in her raked straight stem and flared bow. She had a Gardner 114hp motor and multipurpose mechanically driven winch.

Opposite below: Lead Us II sets out on a herring drifting trip. At other times, she worked flydragging seine-nets, crab and lobster pots, longlines and white fish trawls. She also tried some herring ring-netting but proved too cumbersome for the job.

Lead Us II lies in the Dock End, maybe in 1961 or thereabouts. Alongside her is Danish-type anchor seiner *Ann's* WY178, built in the late 1940s by Whitby Boatbuilding as *Whitehaven* WY178. Anchor seiners hauled their gear broadsides on while lying at anchor, were stalwart and of deep draught to grip the water and maintain position, and had a very full cruiser stern.

Onwards from the mid-1960s, the keelboats developed an increasingly important trawl fishery. Cod in particular congregate around rocks and wrecks. Boats became heftier to pull increasingly robust gear over even rougher ground but were also capable of flydragging seine-net fishing. *Venus* FR79, delivered in 1971 from James Noble (Fraserburgh) Ltd to Skipper Jacob Cole, had beamier lines than earlier keelboats. Her transom stern gave more space aft. Powered by a Gardner 230hp motor, she measured 54ft with 18ft beam, carried a belt-driven seine and trawl winch and a Beccles seine-net rope coiler. In order to handle even weightier trawling gear she was later re-engined with a Volvo Penta 365hp motor with 5:1 reduction gearbox and 55in propeller in a Kort nozzle. Consisting of a cylindrical ring of aerofoil section steel fitted around the propeller, a nozzle gives an increase in trawl pulling power and helps reduce fuel consumption. Big gear reduction ratios and larger diameter, shallow-pitch, slower turning propellers can also improve thrust and allow heavier trawls to be towed.

3

Redcar to Whitby in Colour

Everywhere there is good, strong, rich, clean colour to delight the eye. It enhances the character of the boats and their surrounding paraphernalia.

Built in 1989 by Steve Cook Boatbuilders in Whitby, the mini keelboat *Pride & Joy* WY218 lies ashore for overhaul. Double-ender *The Nagar* came from Tony Goodall in the early 1970s. A nagar is a person born in Runswick Bay.

Built by William
Clarkson, Staithes
double-ender
Radiant Dawn
WY217 is fairly
fine at shoulder
and quarter.
Note the popular
Staithes colours.

Fishing boats were
often berthed
on the esplanade
at Redcar.
Double-ender
Argus MH209
(later *Argos*) was
built by Tony
Goodall in the
1960s for Skipper
Jack Kenyon.

Mini keelboat
Andigee WY372
was delivered in
1993 from Steve
Cook to Skipper
Lee Guy. A small
double-ender lies
alongside.

Above: Jane Elizabeth WY144, built by Whitby Shipbuilding in 1960 for Skipper John Robert Harland, was one of the first cobles in that town to have a wheelhouse.

Right: Courage WY151, built by Goodall in 1986 for Whitby skipper Martin Hopper, was among the last cobles to be fitted with a half-deck.

At Redcar the use of tractors and big axles with pneumatic wheels enabled quite large cobles to be hauled ashore. William Clarkson built the 35ft *Audrey Lass* WY291 in 1978 for brothers Steve and Dean Dandy.

Coble *Daisy Ellen* MH208 was delivered from Gordon Clarkson in the 1960s to the Thompson family at Redcar. More than thirty years later, she was sympathetically restored by former fishing skipper Tony Young.

Curvaceous 26ft double-ender *Seaton Rose* WY310, delivered from Goodall in 1979 to Staithes skipper Frank Hanson, was the favourite of many. One fisherman said, '... the shape of her is how a boat should be.'

Small double-ender *Codwallopers*, produced by Goodall in the 1960s, sits ashore at the foot of 300ft-high cliffs in fog in dilapidated Port Mulgrave, once a shipping place for ironstone.

Owned at Redcar by Colin Barnes, the 18ft *Catriona* MH83 is an attractive example of the double-enders built by Goodall in the 1960s. Compared to Tony's earlier boats she had hollow entry and run, more shoulder and sheer, and finer bilges.

Steel twin-rig trawler *Rebecca* WY790, delivered in 1999 to Lockers Trawlers Ltd from Parkol Marine Engineering Ltd in Whitby, aroused enormous interest. Run by John Oliver and Jim Morrison, Parkol later became one of Britain's most productive builders of fishing vessels.

Rebecca's sister ship *Our Lass* WY797 was handed over from Parkol in 2000 to Lockers. Both were excellent towing boats, which is important to Whitby fishermen who work very heavy trawling gear over rough ground.

Seen across slate and pantile roofs of Whitby in the 1990s, these keelboats lie alongside the fishquay. They are (*left to right*): the trawlers *Kristanjo* WY211, *Headway IV* PD229 (renamed *Rebecca* WY477) and *Orion II* KY118, all belonging to Whitby owners.

Lockers Trawlers had its own net-making and repair department. Tony Price, formerly skipper of *Wakeful* KY261, worked there for a while. Typical Whitby trawls were reinforced with rows of meshes made from thicker twine, both for strength and damage limitation. If part of the net was torn on the unforgiving seabed, the tear should not extend beyond the reinforcements.

Measuring 19ft 6in with 6ft 4in beam, the Skinningrove double-ender *Sheena* WY796 was built by Steve Cook in 1984 as *Anita's Pride* WY52.

4

WHITBY – PART 2

New rules that came into effect in 1980 had a profound influence on the subsequent development of the under 60ft (18.288m) class of boat.

The Merchant Shipping (United Kingdom Fishing Vessels; Manning) Regulation 1980 stipulated that boats below 16.5m (54.133ft) registered length need not have a certificated skipper. The rule formerly applied to boats with a Scottish Part IV Registry of under 25 gross tons. Because this was a measurement of volume, those under 25 tons were restricted in beam and depth in proportion to length. Registered length is measured from the fore side of the rudder stock to the face of the stem, so the new regulations enabled boats of less than 16.5m to be beamier, deeper and fuller than under the 25-ton rule. They could encompass about double the volume with beneficial effects on stability, endurance and fishing capabilities, and were able to carry more top weight such as powerful hauling equipment, steel or aluminium shelterdecks, and spacious living and working accommodation.

The transom-sterned *Sophie Louise* WY168, built by James N. Miller in 1988 for Skipper Howard Locker, was the first large steel trawler specially built for Whitby. Steel has several advantages for fishing boat construction, including strength and resistance to hard knocks from heavy trawl gear. Measuring 59.9ft overall with beam of 22ft and tonnage of 50.81, *Sophie Louise* was built to a chunky, full-bodied, under 16.5m registered length design, with layout arranged to meet Whitby requirements. Her enclosed shelterdeck extended to the port gunwhale, leaving the starboard deck area open for side trawling; a fishing method that gives better manoeuvrability when working heavy gear on restricted areas of craggy ground in strong tides.

Stern trawling was preferable for longer tows, however, with the massive 'scraper' trawl over smooth ground at the Devil's Hole some 150 miles north-east from Whitby. Scrapers were wide, shallow nets designed to catch valuable species such as monkfish, which lie buried in sand. During stern-trawling the warps were towed from gallows at port and starboard quarters, and the scraper net was hauled around a hydraulic net drum aft, as it was too big to be handled on the starboard deck area.

Sophie Louise's Kelvin 495hp 1,315rpm engine drove through a 4:1 reduction gearbox to a 67in-diameter propeller in a Kort nozzle. One of her echo sounders received signals from a transducer fitted on the fishing gear. This helped to indicate the position of the net in relation to seabed obstructions. A fishroom chilling plant kept catches in good condition.

Venus FR79 is launched from the James Noble yard. She was the first transom-sterned boat to be built by the Fraserburgh firm for an English skipper.

In 1972 Mackay Boatbuilders at Arbroath built the 55ft by 18ft cruiser-sterned seiner trawler *Provider* AH71 for Skipper James Storr. Her unusually full lines gave good deck space and carrying capacity. She had a Gardner 230hp, 1,125rpm engine with 3:1 reduction gearbox and her winch was hydraulically powered, which enabled hauling speed to be infinitely variable from inching to maximum.

James N. Miller built the 54ft 6in by 17ft 6in transom-sterned seiner trawler *Lead Us* KY46 in 1972 for Skipper Raymond Storr. She too had a Gardner 230hp motor and hydraulic winch, but she introduced the hydraulic power block to Whitby. *Provider* AH71 lies alongside.

Whitby Shipbuilding went into liquidation in the 1960s but was soon reopened as Whitehall Shipyard. In 1975 it delivered the 55ft by 18ft Scottish-type seiner trawler *Success* LH81 (later WY212) to Skipper James Leadley. By the early 1970s, Whitby had fifteen seiner trawlers whereas only two older keelboats worked pots and lines. Skipper Leadley said, 'Pots, lines and herring nets was a lot of gear. It was simpler to break things down into just two fisheries: seine and trawl.' *Success* was built to lines designed by Scottish naval architects G.L. Watson & Co. She was powered by a Gardner 230hp motor, driving through a 3.5:1 reduction gearbox to the propeller housed in a Kort nozzle. Hydraulically driven gear-handling machinery included a seine and trawl winch and a power block.

Skipper Leadley became very active politically on behalf of British fishermen. He became president of the National Federation of Fishermen's Organisations and was awarded an MBE for his services to the fishing industry.

Opposite above: At 56ft 6in long with 18ft 3in beam, the transom-sterned *Scoresby* FR264, built by Noble in 1978 for Skipper Tal Bennison, was a larger, fuller version of *Venus* FR79 and much more powerful with Kelvin 375hp motor, 3.33:1 reduction gearbox and Kort nozzle, and capable of fishing even deeper ground. She was later renamed *Lead Us Forth* WY235 and then *Jacqueline Louise* WY235.

Opposite below: Robsons Boatbuilders at South Shields built the 55ft Scottish-type seiner trawler *Eskglen* A187 in 1974 for Skipper Robert Peart. She had a Volvo Penta motor. Later, she became *Opportune* WY11.

Scoresby sits on the Fraserburgh slipway ready for completion. In the interests of fish quality, she was the first Whitby boat to have a fishroom chilling plant. She also had sonar, for looking around at seabed obstructions.

Owned by Lockers Trawlers in the 1990s, *Endeavour* WY375 fished under Skipper Michael Locker. The 56ft craft was built in 1978 by Macduff Boatbuilding & Engineering Co. Ltd as *Endeavour II* A297 for Scottish skipper Alec Forsyth. With 18ft beam and tonnage of 24.89, she had been designed below the 25 registered tons ruling for unqualified skippers. She had a 300hp Volvo Penta engine.

Above and below: Sophie Louise WY168 sets out from Whitby. There has been a long association between Scottish boat builders and the Yorkshire port.

Built by J. & G. Forbes & Co. at Sandhaven, Skipper William McPherson's 74ft seiner trawler *Fair Morn* INS 308 sets out from Fraserburgh in 1981 for sea trials. Later she changed hands and became *Resplendent* PD298, working seine-nets from Peterhead. Whitby skipper Richard Brewer bought her in 1997 for single and twin-rig trawling and renamed her *Arrivain III* WY170. She had a Kelvin 495hp engine.

Opposite: Delivered to Skipper David Watt in 1982, the full-bodied 60ft, 470hp Cummins-powered, shelterdecked *Providence* BF422 was Buckie builders Herd & Mackenzie's first boat designed and built in conformance with the below 16.5m ruling. Later fishing as the twin-rigger *Seaway* PD319 under Scottish skipper William Ritchie, she landed prawns and white fish for a while at Whitby around the year 2000.

Skipper George S. Forman's 59ft Kelvin-powered trawler *Jasper II* PD174 sets out from Peterhead. Completed in 1981, she was the final boat built by James Noble (Fraserburgh) Ltd and was later sold to Whitby skipper Richard Brewer. She was also the first in Scotland designed and constructed in compliance with the new below 16.5m registered length criterion for skippers without a seagoing 'ticket'.

By the close of the twentieth century, Whitby's keelboat fleet included several stalwart under 16.5m registered length, pre-owned Scottish-built transom-sterned wooden-hulled white fish and prawn trawlers, with deep and full hull forms and three-quarter length, full-width shelterdecks. Capable of strenuous fishing and chosen for their strong towing features, they had sufficient engine power and fish- and fuel-carrying capacities to make economically worthwhile trips of 350 miles or more. They were able to target unconventional species and yet were sufficiently versatile to take advantage of the occasional prolific local codling fishery. Their full-width shelterdecks permitted stern trawling only. Arnold Locker, director of Lockers Trawlers, which owned several such vessels, said, 'These Scottish boats suit us down to the ground'.

At 16.28m registered length and tonnage of 46.66, the seiner trawler *Orion II* KY118 was built in 1983 by Gerrard Brothers at Arbroath for Skipper William Scott. In 1991 she was re-engined with a Cummins 470hp unit driving the propeller through a 5.335:1 reduction gearbox. Ideal for Whitby needs, she was bought in the mid-1990s by Lockers, who had her fitted with a nozzle and equipped for twin-rig trawling, whereby two nets are towed side by side in order to have a good spread on the seabed and target bottom-living prawns (*Nephrops norvegicus*) and prime flatfish. A three-drum trawl winch was installed because the gear is towed by three trawl warps rather than two.

Coming below 16.5m registered length, the capacious 61.66ft by 22ft trawler *Ocean Way* WY785 was delivered from Macduff Boatbuilding early in 1987 as *Atlas* BF245 to Skipper William West. Her registered tonnage of 46.31 was almost double that of comparable boats of similar length built prior to 1981 for skippers without seagoing tickets, and she was some 4ft greater in the beam. She had a Caterpillar 400hp motor. Later fitted with a Kort nozzle and equipped for twin-rigging, she fished as *Ocean Way* BF64. Bought by Lockers in the late 1990s and fishing under Skipper Richard Marsay in the year 2000, she worked the twin-rig to good effect on the Dogger Bank and caught much plaice and lemon sole.

At other times, *Orion II* and *Ocean Way* would work tough, heavy single-net trawling gear anywhere in the North Sea, depending on where the fish was. A typical Whitby four-panel rockhopper trawl had panels let into its sides, which gave it a high opening to catch haddock and whiting in addition to cod and flatfish. Rubber discs, or 'rockhoppers', on the groundrope were designed to bounce over rocks to reduce the likelihood of net snagging. Both boats also caught high-value red mullet, which was beginning to figure seriously on Whitby fish market.

Orion II KY118 comes into Whitby's upper harbour. Fishing under Skipper David Price in 2001, she enjoyed a particularly good red mullet fishery.

Atlas BF245 lies in Macduff harbour following a repaint. Later she became *Ocean Way* BF64 and then moved to Whitby as *Ocean Way* WY785.

Opposite above: Steel twin-rig trawler *Rebecca* WY790, delivered in 1999 to Lockers Trawlers from Parkol Marine Engineering Ltd in Whitby, was an excellent towing boat. She constantly outfished other vessels of a similar size and aroused enormous interest. Her Caterpillar 480hp, 1,800rpm engine with 5.5:1 reduction gear drove the propeller housed in a Kort nozzle.

Opposite below: Rebecca's crew of Whitby lads were (*from left to right, standing*): Skipper Michael Locker, Chris Hall, John Harland and John Storr; (*in the foreground*) Arnold Locker's son James Locker as trainee skipper.

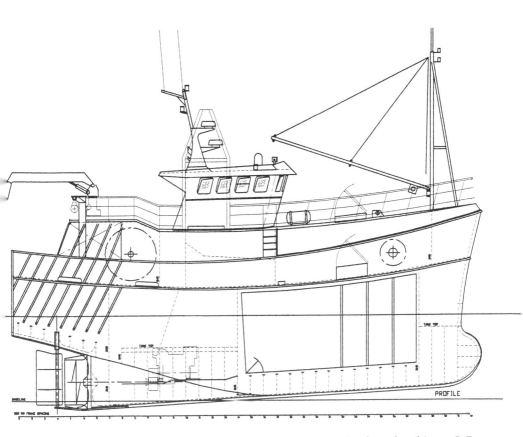

Designed to her owners' requirements by Ian Paton MRINA of naval architects S.C. McAllister & Co. Ltd, *Rebecca* was 59ft 11in long overall with 16.5m registered length. Her massive 23ft beam probably made her the most spacious 60ft craft yet built. *General Arrangement drawing, courtesy S.C. McAllister & Company Ltd*

Opposite above: Our Lass WY797, delivered from Parkol in 2000 to Lockers Trawlers, was in most respects a repeat of *Rebecca* but had a 6:1 reduction gearbox and larger nozzle and propeller for even better towing strength. She carried more fuel, wheelhouse instruments were largely of a different make, and minor adjustments were made to her deck layout. Skipper James Locker, formerly with *Rebecca*, took command.

Opposite below: Our Lass under construction. Note the framework for her semi-bulbous bow. This prominent feature gave a longer keel length to improve her directional stability and towing efficiency. The Parkol boats were constructed from ready-cut steel components delivered in kit form from other suppliers.

Plating under way on *Our Lass* shows her round bilges and the form of the semi-bulbous bow. Relatively fine forward lines provided a good water flow to the propeller in the interests of towing capabilities.

Two keelboats and a nice group of cobles lie alongside the fishquay, sometime in the early 1970s. Keelboat *Provider* AH71 lies next to the quay. Alongside her is the cruiser-sterned seiner trawler *C.K.S.* KY47 delivered from Smith & Hutton in 1973 to Skipper George Storr. Cobles were still the mainstay of the static gear fleet at this time.

Gordon Clarkson, who set up business in 1950, said, 'Engines were getting more powerful and cobles needed more beam. I started the trend with beamier cobles such as *Sea Harvest* with her fullness carried forward and a beam of 9ft 6in.' Built in 1957 for Skipper David Peart, *Sea Harvest* WY115 was 32ft 6in long with a 15hp Petter diesel engine.

C.A. Goodall built the 30ft 8in by 9ft 10in coble *Sea Vispur* WY17 in the late 1960s for Whitby owner James Purvis. Note the stout oak beams ready to receive the planking for the half-deck. *Vispur* was an anagram of her owner's surname. She was powered by a Lister 36hp diesel motor. In 1971 she foundered and became a total loss.

Some cobles from Gordon Clarkson were slighter in shape. Whitby skipper Louis Breckon, who had the 33ft *Alliance* WY39 built in 1971, often worked longlines and believed that a finer-lined coble was easier to handle. Louis said, 'She had a tight turn.'

Larger cobles from Gordon Clarkson in the 1970s included the half-decked *Hannah Mary* WY84, handed over in 1973 to Whitby brothers Alfred and Richard Wastell. Named after their mother, *Hannah Mary* measured 34ft 6in with 10ft 6in beam and was powered by a Lister 45hp diesel engine.

By the 1980s many cobles had small wheelhouses. Shapely 32ft 2in by 10ft 4.5in *Winnie S* SN33 was delivered in 1985 from Goodall to Skipper John Stocks of Cullercoats. Should she work from the beach, her Lister 46.25hp air-cooled engine could be started before she entered the water.

Winnie S was particularly full in the head and had the reputation of '… throwing the water away from her'. Later changing hands, she worked pots and nets for a while out of Whitby under Skipper Barry Tose.

Since the 1970s, inclement weather and the growing use of hydraulic machinery for hauling fishing gear caused cobles to be fitted with more powerful motors. The 32ft 7in by 10ft 6in half-decked *Courage* WY151, built by Goodall in 1986 for Skipper Martin Hopper, had a marinised C-Power Ford 77hp, 2,600rpm diesel engine. Martin specialised in longline fishing for cod on hard ground.

Skipper Martin Hopper (*left*), with boat builders Tony Goodall (*centre*) and Maurice Brown. Tony set up business at Sandsend in 1953 and, by the time he retired in 1995, had produced more than thirty cobles and numerous double-enders. Maurice worked with him for some twenty years.

Boat builders in the Whitby area built many cobles for elsewhere. Jack Lowther delivered the 28ft *Rain-Goose* SN79 in 1973 to North Shields. She was powered by a Ford 72hp diesel engine with direct drive gearbox.

Steve Cook built *Energy* SH105 in 1987 for Filey owners Richard and Nigel Cammish. Steve said, 'The drafts of beach cobles should be as flat as you can get them, to float in as little water as possible. Drafts and forefoot should grip the beach at the same time.' *Energy* had an 80hp Ford engine with 1.5:1 reduction gearbox.

Many static gear boats based at Whitby in the late twentieth century were fully decked non-local types built in wood, steel or fibreglass. Known as mini keelboats, they were roomier than cobles, able to work further afield in worse weather, and could carry more fishing gear and bigger catches.

Whitby builders produced some rugged wooden-hulled, heavy displacement, transom-sterned mini keelboats. Steve Cook built several for Whitby and elsewhere, although none were exactly alike in shape. 'They are general purpose fishing boats,' Steve said, '... able to do trawling, potting, lining and netting. They are very full beamy boats with full round bilges and a deep draught which is a good stability feature and enables us to make a big propeller aperture.'

During the 1980s boats measuring 10m registered length or under did not require Pressure Stock Licences and were exempt from individual catch limitations. Skipper Keith Wilson's 35ft 127hp Gardner-powered potter and netter *Pride & Joy* WY218, handed over from Steve in 1989, had a registered length below 10m.

Opposite above: Coming below 10m registered length, the 35ft 6in by 14ft 6in, 180hp Ford-powered *Bold Venture III* BH234, delivered from Steve in 1990 to Amble skipper Michael Bould, was slightly beamier and deeper than *Pride & Joy*, with more sheer and broader transom, flatter less hollow floors, and lower, fuller bilges. A bigger propeller aperture accommodated a 36in-diameter propeller, which, together with a 4:1 reduction gear, gave good thrust for trawling.

Opposite below: During 1990 the cut-off point for Pressure Stock Licences changed to 10m length overall and below. Amble skipper Geoffrey Burge's trawler and netter *Incentive* BH243, which came from Steve in 1992, was shorter than *Bold Venture III* to fall below 10m overall and, consequently, was stockier. She had a Ford 180hp, 2,600rpm motor with 4:1 reduction gear.

Measuring below 10m long overall, the exceptionally tough and full-bodied gill and trammel netter *Rose Anne* WY164, built by Steve in 1992 for Skipper Roger Thoelen, was a whopper of a mini keelboat. Her 15ft beam was almost half her 32ft 8in overall length. She was powered by a Mermaid Ford-based 180hp diesel engine with 3:1 reduction gearbox.

Opposite above: Mini keelboat *Andigee* WY372 hauls crab and lobster pots. Delivered from Steve in 1993 she was 32ft 8in long overall but, at the request of Skipper Lee Guy, was only 13ft on the beam with 5ft 2in draught, so she was leaner and sparer than the portly *Rose Anne*. Her Mermaid Ford engine provided 180hp at 2,600rpm with 3:1 reduction gear.

Opposite below: The 34ft 6in potter, netter and longliner *Silver Line W* WY68, built by Jack Lowther for Skipper Harold Winspear in 1988, was a full-bodied mini keelboat designed to escape the 1980s pressure stock regime with registered length below 10m. Powered by a Gardner 127hp motor, she had 13ft 8in beam and 4ft 6in draught.

Opposite above: Carvel-planked 32ft 8in by 14ft, below 10m length overall, mini keelboat *Bread Winner* WY367, handed over from Lowther in 1992 to Skipper Richard Marsay, carried her fullness well forward and aft. She worked pots, longlines, gill and trammel nets, and white fish and prawn trawls. Fittings included a Cummins 220hp engine and a Koden Chromascope echo sounder, which displayed echoes in eight colours according to the nature of the target.

Opposite below: *Rose Anne* WY164 was beamier and deeper than *Incentive* BH243, with a wider transom to give ample space for storing nets aft. Skipper Roger Thoelen was pleased with *Rose Anne* and said, 'She's put some rough weather away. We've hauled the gear in winds up to Force seven and eight.'

Bread Winner WY367 was in fact built by Jack Lowther's son John. Jack was retiring after thirty-two years in business and said, 'All my boats were full in the head. I built a dinghy when I was sixteen but she turned out finer lined than what I wanted. Even in those days I thought a full boat was a good idea.'

There were happenings and diversions. Early in 1994 the small Whitby trawler *Selina Ann* NN88 was left behind by the receding tide on rocks at the foot of towering cliffs near Staithes, after her engine had overheated and been shut down. She was refloated on the next tide.

There are those who try something different. Skipper Walter Walker built the 32ft steel catamaran *Steelaway* WY364 near his cliff-top home at Port Mulgrave. Her launch in 1995, down 300ft-high cliffs into the isolated and ramshackle harbour, involved the use of pulleys, hawsers, earth-moving machinery and enthusiastic volunteer helpers. Onlookers came from many parts.

Above and below: During the 1990s hundreds of British boats were broken up under the European Union's decommissioning programme, whereby fishermen were compensated financially for removing their vessels from the fishing fleets. While it was broadly realised that overfishing should be curbed, robust fishermen broke down in tears at the savage destruction of many attractive craft.

Many cobles met their end. The Goodall-built *Darren S* WY113 became a woeful little heap of timber and twisted metal. Although, under EU rules, decommissioned boats could be transferred to a third country or found some non-fishing purposes, the United Kingdom demanded that they be destroyed or otherwise permanently disabled.

Opposite above: There were happier circumstances. In 2001 Scottish skipper Karl Phimister took delivery of the below 16.5m registered length twin-rig trawler *Reliant* BCK101 from Parkol. Her lines were based on those of *Rebecca* WY790 and *Our Lass* WY797, but her transom raked aft to give a bigger overall length. She was slightly fuller aft for additional buoyancy and her keel deeper to accommodate larger propeller and nozzle. *Reliant* was Caterpillar-powered with a 7:1 reduction ratio gearbox.

Opposite below: Reliant was constructed from pre-cut steel components supplied by Steel-Kit Ltd. An underwater plasma cutting technique cut the steel accurately and reduced heat distortion. Having the framework and plates ready for construction eliminated the need for small yards to have costly steel-forming equipment.

Reliant is ready to be lifted into the River Esk by a huge crane, which towers over Whitby. Under the directorship of marine engineer John Oliver and welder and fabricator Jim Morrison, Parkol went on to become one of Whitby's great triumphs. Today, in 2013, it ranks among Britain's foremost boatyards, having built twenty-five steel commercial fishing vessels of high quality for places as far apart as Cornwall and the Shetland Islands. They have included scallopers, single-net and twin-rig trawlers, vivier crabbers and a gill netter, all designed by naval architect Ian Paton to the requirements of their owners and equipped with close attention to detail and particular needs. Sadly, in 2010, John Oliver died. A thoughtful and friendly man, he was held in high regard.

Lockers Trawlers has placed the order for a 25m (82ft) fully shelterdecked white fish trawler, in which emphasis will be placed on fuel efficiency, speed, seakeeping qualities and carrying capacity.

Opposite above: In 2010 Parkol handed over the 23.3m (76ft) by 7.2m (23ft) prawn and white fish twin-rig trawler *Virtuous* FR253 to Fraserburgh skippers Sandy West and Keith Buchan. Propulsion characteristics and a number of design innovations have given her good towing capabilities combined with big savings in fuel consumption. She has a Mitsubishi 1,350rpm engine with 7:1 reduction gearbox. Note her double-chine hull form.

Opposite below: Skilled sign writer Paul Robinson paints imaginative stem crests on the Parkol vessels. The stem crest on *Virtuous* shows a map of Scotland and the Saltire flag set within a Scottish thistle.

Seen here in Fraserburgh following her completion in 1969, cruiser-sterned trawler *Ocean Reward* FR28 was built by James Noble for Bridlington skipper Jack Sanderson. Thirty years later, she was sold to a retired solicitor who wished to live on board her. Sympathetic conversion was carried out in Whitby by Parkol.

Parkol has full repair and refit facilities. *Magdalene Ann* SH33 is here having a repaint. A superb example of a classic Scottish, wooden-hulled, cruiser-sterned boat, the 45ft craft was built in Girvan by Alexander Noble & Sons Ltd as *Magdalene Ann* CT33 for Isle of Man owners.

5

REDCAR, MARSKE AND SKINNINGROVE

At Redcar the coast is low and sandy. In the 1990s, a small and lively commercial inshore fishery continued to operate from the beach here, on a full or part-time basis.

Cobles and double-enders appear to have been equally fitted for similar purposes. There are those who prefer a double-ender. Skipper David Marshall, of the 24ft *Patricia Christine* WY53, said:

> A double-ender is a lot easier than a coble to handle on the beach. She can come in through almost anything and get as near as damnit out of the water. Cobles are easier to launch because they do it bow first but a double-ender can turn round inside the surf if you time it right and then face the waves. But you must take care. There tend to be seven big waves and then a bit of calm.

David said that, whereas a 27ft coble could carry forty pots, *Patricia Christine* can hold eighty.

With 8ft 9.5in beam, *Patricia Christine* was built by Goodall in 1984 and is somewhat similar in hull form to *Seaton Rose* WY310 at Staithes. Goodall double-enders had evolved in shape. Tony's younger brother Leslie, who worked at the Sandsend yard for a while, said:

> Our early double-enders carried their flat bottoms a long way forward and aft and the garboard strakes were full at their ends. The idea was to float in very shallow water, but the propeller was not sufficiently immersed. So we created a different shape. We made the entry and run finer and more hollow to produce a wine-glass shape in the end sections and shorter flat mid sections.

We also eased the bilges slightly to give an easier waterline. As a result, the boats sat in rather than on the water and the redesigned entry and run gave a clean water flow to make the best use of the small propeller. We also made the boats a little fuller at shoulder and quarter and also gave the stem more rake which helped create hollowness and flare.

In Goodall's early double-enders, powered by outboard engines, depth aft was restricted by the standard length of the motor shaft. Later, an increase in shaft length enabled the boats to be deeper aft with more sheer. The growing use of inboard engines allowed the vessels' form to evolve still further, resulting in fuller, beamier craft, which had greater sea range and were capable of carrying more fishing gear and hauling machinery.

The fully developed hull form was described by Tony Goodall:

Shoulders and quarters are full for carrying capacity, and the slightly finer hollow entry prevents blashing [slamming]. Together with a slightly raked stem the hollow entry gives us the chance to make a nice flared bow for seakeeping and a nice appearance. A slightly S-shaped sheer gives height at the shoulders

Rebel Maid (*above and right*) and *Laurie D* (*opposite*) show the evolution in the hull form of double-enders built by Tony Goodall. Designed to float in very shallow water, the 16ft 6in by 5ft 9in *Rebel Maid* was built in 1958 for Redcar owner Mrs Alford and powered by oar and outboard motor. Her garboard strakes are quite full at their ends.

Built in 1985 for Redcar garage owner Ian Denney, the 18ft by 6ft *Laurie D* has finer, hollower entry and run, and fuller shoulders and quarters, than *Rebel Maid*. She has easier waterline, greater depth aft than forward, and a stronger sheer. She was designed for propulsion by a 10hp Yanmar inboard motor. Her sawn frames are similar to those in a coble.

where they take the seas first. The full bow enables them to run before a sea without burying their heads.

Because the engine is aft they sit lower at the quarters when under way. So we give them more height aft than forward. This, together with full quarters, also gives lift and prevents water spilling in during beaching and launching. There is slight tumblehome at the top two strakes for seaworthiness and less weight. The slightly rockered keel improves the boats' landing capabilities when coming ashore onto the beach and trailer. It is important that the drafts are parallel to the keel so they will travel freely onto the axle.

The largest double-ender at Redcar in the mid-1990s was Skipper Michael Haydon's 26ft by 9ft 6in *Valiant Star* H73, built in the 1980s by Steve Cook. As Michael recalled, 'She was 6ft 8in high aft, higher than forward for taking the breakers when coming in.' Steve said, 'My double-enders are full aft for lifting when the waves come, and they draw more water aft. They pull and move to the fishing gear very well. They have a little bit of tumblehome and the keel is slightly rockered.' *Valiant Star* had a Perkins 56hp diesel motor and a few sawn frames interspersed with steam bent timbers. She worked six fleets of gill nets for cod.

Some 8 miles south-east from Redcar lies the gritty and desolate one-time ironstone-mining village of Skinningrove, where the beck runs orange with contamination from the old mine workings. The beach is softer than at Redcar, with shifting sands offshore and much seaweed and debris.

Skinningrove double-enders had air-cooled engines because they could be started before the vessels were afloat, and thus had no cooling intakes to clog up with silt and weed. Steve Cook built the 19ft 6in by 6ft 4in *Anita's Pride* WY52 in 1984 for Skinningrove. Later renamed *Sheena* WY796, she worked gill nets for cod and 200 crab and lobster pots. Her owner said, 'She's a wide little boat with plenty of bottom to sit in the water well. She doesn't roll and was built to last with excellent workmanship.' *Sheena* had been re-engined with a 13hp Lister air-cooled motor.

One of the earliest of Tony Goodall's new model of double-ender was the 21ft *Aytonia* WY229, built in 1966 for Staithes but later fishing from Skinningrove as *Lisa M* WY229. She carried her original Lister air-cooled engine. Tony kept record of the basic details of his boats, including plank widths at various positions, to give some guidance when arriving at the required shape in later vessels (see p. 112), but few boats were exactly alike. New owners would state their preference according to existing vessels but would ask for modifications, thereby bringing about a continuous evolution in line and detail. For instance, more beam could be created by increasing the width of one or two bottom planks.

Built in 1959 for Skipper Bryan Maude, the 22ft Redcar double-ender *Lady Maude* MH150 was based on Tony Goodall's earlier concepts with her garboard strakes full at their ends. She had a Brit 10hp petrol inboard engine.

Above: Hope MH103, built in the 1960s by Goodall, has the new shape with hollow entry and run, easier waterline and a more pronounced sheer. The 18ft craft originally belonged to Staithes but later moved to Redcar.

Below: In 2001 *Lisa M* WY229 worked pots from Skinningrove and still had her original Lister air-cooled diesel motor. Built by Goodall as *Aytonia* WY229 in 1966, she was one of the first built to his reshaped basic design.

Gardenia II MH202 comes ashore at Redcar. Measuring 21.2ft, she was handed over in 1966 to Skipper William Gardner and embodied her builder's new ideas in hull form, which made for a very attractive boat.

A page from Tony Goodall's notebook shows basic particulars of the double-ender *Aytonia*. The plank widths gave some guidance when Tony came to build similar boats at a later date.

Tony continued to develop the new fundamental design of his double-enders in keeping with owners' requirements. *Argus* MH209 (later *Argos*), built *c.* 1968 for Redcar skipper Jack Kenyon, was similar to *Gardenia II* MH202 but shorter and somewhat stockier at 20ft 10in long.

In the mid-1960s, Goodall built the 19ft double-ender *Little Pal* MH2 for Redcar skipper Bob Walton. He said, 'The big problem here is the size of the seas near to shore, and if she comes through that you know you've got a good boat. She just seems to throw the seas away and doesn't care about it.'

Patricia Christine WY53, built by Goodall in 1984, is a much-admired double-ender. Redcar skipper Dave Marshall said, 'We use 400 pots and work from close inshore behind the rocks to three or four miles out.' She has sawn oak frames.

Patricia Christine's Leyland 33hp, 2,500rpm, water-cooled diesel engine drove the 18in-diameter propeller via a gearbox of 2:1 reduction ratio. Tony Goodall referred to his double-enders as '… wooden clinker-built double-headed surfboats'.

Above: Built in 1993, the 24ft by 8ft 5in double-ender *Flora Jane* WY251 was the final full-time fishing boat from Tony Goodall before he retired in 1995. Similar in style to *Patricia Christine*, she carried a 36hp motor and pot and gill net haulers. Owner Peter Lince said, 'This size of boat is right for Redcar. At sea she moves about more quickly than a coble.'

Below: Rather than having steam-bent timbers, *Flora Jane* had sawn frames similar to those in a coble. They were joggled and bevelled to fit against the clinker planking. Here, Maurice Brown works on a frame. Tony valued Maurice's skilled help hugely and said, 'He was my right-hand man. We worked as a team.'

Opposite above: Built by Scarborough Marine Engineers in 1998 for Filey and later bought by Redcar fisherman John Atherton, *Isis* SH278 measured 26ft by 8ft 6in with a 72hp Ford engine. John said, 'I wanted a double-ender as big as I could find. She responds well ... a coble has no steerage in the surf until her rudder is in place but a double-ender has her rudder on all the time.'

Opposite below: In her shape, *Isis* was based on the large double-ender *Janet & Carol* SH229 built by Gordon Clarkson in Whitby. Gordon said that double-enders should be full bodied enough for carrying but finer at their ends so they don't bang themselves up and down like a frying pan.

Skipper Michael Haydon's 26ft double-ender *Valiant Star* H73 is towed ashore at Redcar. Built by Steve Cook in the 1980s, she is full and high aft for coping with the breakers when approaching the beach. Note the big net hauler. *Valiant Star* worked six fleets of gill nets, mainly for cod. For small boats, double-enders were excellent weight carriers.

Along the coast a mile or so south-east of Redcar is Marske-by-the-Sea. Double-enders are popular here where the seas are short and steep, and break on the offshore sandbanks. Fishermen speak highly of double-enders built by Pickersgill & Sons Ltd of Thornaby-on-Tees. These had full shoulders and quarters, low round bilges and broad flat bottoms, closely spaced oak timbers, fine entry and run, and some tumblehome. They were built 'on the ram': a thick central plank to which were fastened the garboard strakes on either side. The keel, fitted last, was chiefly there to act as an expendable member protecting the hull's bottom on the beach. Protective rubbing strips were fitted below the lands of the strakes for much or all of their length.

Bill Goodwill at Marske was very proud of his 22.2ft *Moonraker* built by Pickersgill *c.* 1960. He said that Ned Kieser, Pickersgill's master boat builder, '… produced marvellous sea boats; they were masterpieces, works of art for the sea'.

Opposite above: Bill Goodwill said of *Moonraker*, 'She has tumblehome. She is wider underneath than on top and can lean over in a sea without shipping water.'

Opposite below: One of Pickersgill's final double-enders was *Mary Oakley* MH162, built in 1961 as a sea angling boat for blast furnace manager Arthur Embleton. Double-enders made ideal recreational and part-time commercial fishing craft in the ironstone-mining and steel-making communities. *Mary Oakley* was a bit deeper than *Moonraker* and slacker in the bilge with a narrower bottom.

This retired double-ender sits on a roundabout in Redcar. She was built by Pickersgill shortly after the Second World War for a man who planned to take holidaymakers on pleasure trips from Redcar beach. For this purpose she was roomy with a broad, flat bottom to accommodate passengers, and her shallow draught would enable her to float at the water's edge while people walked along mobile gangways to board and disembark. Running trips to sea was a profitable business in the early post-war years. Holidaymakers flocked to the British seaside. In the event, the original purchase of the 21ft boat fell through, and she was later bought by brothers Peter and George White, named *Volente* MH42, and used for commercial fishing with pots and longlines.

Above: Some Redcar men preferred cobles. At 32.9ft, *Maria Cristina* MH157 was built by Gordon Clarkson in 1960 for Skipper Garry Mountain. The wheelhouse was a later addition.

Below: In 1973 Jack Lowther was fully occupied in building cobles in his new 80ft shed, in which three of the craft could be constructed simultaneously. Measuring 27.5ft, *Manuela* MH118 was built for Redcar skipper John Barry Davies. She had 42hp BMC engine.

Lowther delivered the 31ft 10in by 9ft 8in coble *Silver Jubilee* WY268 in 1977 to Skipper Eric Smithson. Designed to her owner's requirements, she had deep forefoot and shallow drafts to keep her straight when making a landing through shallow water. Eric said, 'You need bow and stern to touch the beach together. I also asked for less sheer aft for ease of climbing in and out when setting off and coming ashore. She was a good sea boat with full shoulder for carrying pots.'

Silver Jubilee's Ford 80hp, 2,500rpm motor had a direct drive gearbox so the propeller could be small enough to be housed between the shallow drafts. The wheelhouse was added later, and a Ford 120hp replacement engine gave sufficient power for trawling.

Opposite above: Skipper Ken Rolph's 34ft coble *Freedom* WY271, produced by Gordon Clarkson in 1977, had 10ft 3in beam and an 80hp motor. She originally had no wheelhouse and used a canvas 'dodger' erected forward from stem to engine area.

Opposite below: Built by Goodall in 1982 for Redcar skipper Ted Price, the 28ft by 8ft 9in coble *Jane Marie* WY337 was powered by a Ford 56hp, 2,250rpm engine with 1.5:1 reduction gearbox. Ted Price said, 'Cobles are sturdy and take a lot of punishment.'

Early in 1984, Goodall delivered the 30ft by 9ft 10in *Gentle Barbara II* WY17 to Skipper Ernest Thomas. She ran her trials in Whitby. Tony said, 'These Redcar cobles must not be too big and heavy as there is some manhandling involved.'

Above: Gentle Barbara II is towed along the road in Redcar to her berth in Fisherman's Square. She had a Mercedes-Benz 80hp, 2,600rpm engine with 1.5:1 reduction ratio and 19in-diameter propeller.

Below: Gentle Barbara II under construction at Sandsend. Tony said that Redcar cobles '… need to be handy, with smaller drafts and able to be launched and recovered quickly. It is important that their drafts are parallel and vertical so that they will travel freely onto the axle without causing stress to the hull.'

Opposite above: The 27ft *Suvera* MH276, built by Goodall in 1978 for Skipper Paul Wilson, had leaner lines than *Gentle Barbara II* and 8ft 4in beam. Paul said, 'She's small and light enough to get in and out of the water quickly. The beach is soft so you can't mess about or you'll get bogged down.'

Opposite below: The 180th boat built by Tony Goodall since he set up business in 1953 was the stout, 32ft 6in by 11ft 3in coble *Incentive* WY373, delivered in 1992 to Redcar skipper Adrian Turnbull. Tony was asked to build her hull only. Adrian took her elsewhere for fitting out.

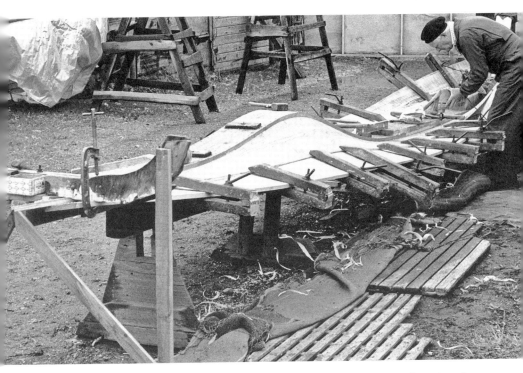

Incentive was the final coble from Goodall. Here, Tony works on the bottom strakes. Note the raised ram tunnel under which the propeller will be accommodated. Planking the tunnel requires enormous skill and produces one of the most unusual shapes in wooden boat building.

Above: Incentive under construction. Very few cobles are exactly alike in line and detail. Adrian Turnbull wanted one similar to *Charisma* WY313 but asked for greater beam and less tumblehome to provide space for gill nets, and shallow drafts for working from the beach.

Below: Tony (*left*) and Maurice shape the oak side frames for *Incentive*. Oak is tough, durable and strong, and can be obtained with a natural sweep of grain from which to cut curved components such as frames. The planks are of larch, which is straight grained and abrasion resistant.

Some things at Redcar were out of the ordinary. Cobles had Latin words and phrases painted on their sterns. That on *Suvera* MH276 read '*SPIRITU SANCTI*', which translates as 'Holy Spirit'.

A good number of small cobles and some double-enders were of glass-reinforced-plastic construction. Richard W.S. Cole at Lythe near Whitby produced the sturdy 19ft 3in Redcar-based GRP double-ender *Jade Katrice* MH226 for Skipper Ron Horseman, who chose the material for its low-maintenance properties.

POSTSCRIPT

When the keelboat *Venus* FR79 arrived in Whitby in 1971 her up-to-dateness caused a stir. She fished well. Skipper Jake Cole had a good knowledge of the inshore trawling grounds and one stretch of seabed was known as Jake's Garden.

Today, in 2013, *Venus* lies obliquely threadbare upriver from Whitby, but there are plans to convert her into a houseboat.

Just downriver from where *Venus* awaits her future, boat builder Steve Cook has continued to use his considerable expertise. Sometime around 2008 he built the agreeable little 18ft wooden double-ender *Sea Moon II*, for an owner who works a few crab and lobster pots from Runswick Bay. Superlative traditional boat-building skills are not yet lost in the Whitby area.

GLOSSARY

There may be those who read this book that are new to the fishing industry and boat design. This glossary may be of interest to them.

Beam	The maximum width of the boat.
Bilge	That part of the boat where the bottom turns upwards to become the sides.
Bow, or bows, and stern	The forward and after parts of the boat.
Canoe stern	A sharp-ended counter, which rakes aft at the centre line and has its fullest part at the toprail.
Carvel planking	Planking fitted edge to edge.
Clinker planked	The planks overlap.
Counter	The overhanging part of the stern where it extends abaft the rudder.
Cruiser stern	A sharp-ended counter, which rakes forward at the centre-line and has its fullest part at or below the waterline.
Draught	Depth to which the boat is immersed.
Drift-net	Sheets of netting are joined end to end and hung vertically in the path of oncoming fish, which are caught in the mesh by their gills.

Entry	The forward part of the boat below the waterline.
Flare	Outward curvature of the boat above the waterline.
Floors	Structural members lying across the keel, or across the ram plank in cobles, and continuous with the frames on either side.
Flydragging seine-net	This uses a funnel-shaped net attached to the boat by long ropes. The vessel hauls the ropes, which converge and herd the fish into the path of the net.
Forefoot	The lower part of the stem where it curves to join the keel.
Garboard strake	The strake adjacent to the keel.
Gunwhale	The uppermost length of timber along both sides of the hull, usually standing proud of the sheerstrake and the frames or timbers.
Hard, firm or full bilges	Round bilges with a tight turn.
Heavy displacement	Weighty; displacing quite a lot of water.
Hollow	Concave.
Hull	The body or shell of the boat, excluding fittings and superstructure.
Lands	Plank overlaps.
Pressure Stock Licences	Licences that permit the capture of species considered to be at risk of overfishing and subject to quota restrictions.
Quarters	The after ends of the boat's sides.
Raked	Inclined from the vertical.
Ring-net	This encloses herring shoals in sheltered waters and is worked by two boats.
Rockered	Curved fore and aft.
Run	The after part of the boat below the water.
Sheer	Longitudinal curvature of the boat's top strake.

Sheerstrake	The uppermost strake.
Shoulders	The forward ends of the boat's sides.
Side trawling	Working the nets and warps from one side of the vessel.
Siding	The width of a piece of timber.
Slack, easy, soft or fine bilges	A more relaxed as opposed to a hard curve to the bilges in cross section.
Static gear	Fishing gear that is anchored to the seabed, including crab and lobster pots, longlines, gill nets and trammel nets. Trammel nets consist of three parallel vertical sheets of netting. A gill net comprises one sheet of netting.
Stem	The forward limit of the boat's centreline structure.
Stern trawling	Working the gear over the stern.
Strake	One complete length of planking from stem to stern.
Timbers	Transverse ribs steam-bent to shape.
Transom stern	The after part of the boat that ends square.
Trawl	Trawling employs a funnel-shaped net attached to the boat by wire warps. As it is towed through the water, it is kept open by floats and weights and otter boards.
Tumblehome	Inward slope of the upper sides of the boat.